Inventory of Amphibians and Reptiles of George Washington Birthplace National Monument

Technical Report NPS/NER/NRTR-2008/110

Joseph C. Mitchell, Ph. D.

Department of Biology
University of Richmond
Richmond, VA 23173

March 2008
U.S. Department of the Interior
National Park Service
Northeast Region
Philadelphia, Pennsylvania

The Northeast Region of the National Park Service (NPS) comprises national parks and related areas in 13 New England and Mid-Atlantic states. The diversity of parks and their resources are reflected in their designations as national parks, seashores, historic sites, recreation areas, military parks, memorials, and rivers and trails. Biological, physical, and social science research results, natural resource inventory and monitoring data, scientific literature reviews, bibliographies, and proceedings of technical workshops and conferences related to 38 of these park units in Maryland, New Jersey, Pennsylvania, Virginia, and West Virginia are disseminated through the NPS/NERCHAL Technical Report and Natural Resources Report series. The reports are a continuation of series with previous acronyms of NPS/PHSO and NPS/MAR, although they retain a consecutive numbering system. Individual parks may also disseminate information through their own report series.

Mention of trade names or commercial products does not constitute endorsement or recommendation for use by the National Park Service.

This technical report was produced by the University of Richmond under Cooperative Agreement 4560-B-0003, Supplemental Agreement No. 2, with the Northeast Region.

Reports in these series are produced in limited quantities and, as long as the supply lasts, may be obtained by sending a request to the address on the back cover. When original quantities are exhausted, copies may be requested from the NPS Technical Information Center (TIC), Denver Service Center, PO Box 25287, Denver, CO 80225-0287. A copy charge may be involved. To order from TIC, refer to document D-360.

This report may also be available as a downloadable portable document format file from the Internet at www.nps.gov/nero/science.

Please cite this publication as:

Mitchell, J. C. March 2008. Inventory of Amphibians and Reptiles of George Washington Birthplace National Monument. National Park Service, Northeast Region. Philadelphia, PA. Natural Resources Report NPS/NER/NRTR-2008/110. http://www.nps.gov/nero/science

NPS D-360 March 2008

Table of Contents

Figures

Tables

Appendices

Executive Summary

This inventory was conducted at George Washington Birthplace National Monument (GEWA) in 2002 and 2003, to 1) document 90% of the amphibians (frogs, salamanders) and reptiles (turtles, lizards, snakes) of GEWA, 2) describe their associated habitats, and 3) provide park staff with conservation and management recommendations. Survey methods included visual encounter surveys, audio surveys, and road surveys; dipnets, minnow traps, and turtle traps.

Thirteen species of frogs, 11 salamander species, seven turtle species, six lizard species, and 15 snake species were expected to occur at GEWA based on known distribution patterns in published literature. The proportion of species documented during this inventory, based on the expected species list, was 62% for frogs, 36% for salamanders, 100% for turtles, 50% for lizards, and 40% for snakes. Total success was 54% of expected species for amphibians and 57% for reptiles. These success levels are reasonable based on similar inventories conducted elsewhere in Virginia, and sampling limitations caused by the drought conditions that prevailed during the first two years of the study.

Nine habitat types used by amphibians and reptiles at GEWA were described from the field notes obtained during this inventory, and include beach, grassland, marsh, mixed hardwoods and pine, mixed hardwoods, mixed pine, impoundments, swamp, and stream. All habitats surveyed support multiple species, and most species use both aquatic and terrestrial habitat types. Habitats that support relatively unique assemblages include hardwood forests, tidal marshes, and vernal pools. Only one species is habitat-specific, the Diamond-backed Terrapin (*Malaclemys terrapin terrapin*) in the estuarine marsh. The combination of habitat types used by amphibians and reptiles at GEWA should be viewed as a matrix of habitats imbedded within the landscape rather than as separate habitat types, and should be protected as such.

Although this study documented less than 90% of the expected number of species for several groups, there are opportunities to register additional species. This can be accomplished in two ways by park staff: routine accumulation of digital photographs of road-kills or live amphibians and reptiles encountered with appropriate documentation appended to the digital image, and the use of natural history (animal) sighting cards filled out by knowledgeable visitors. Verification of new species records should be confirmed by a herpetologist.

Recommendations for GEWA resource management include: (1) Additional species inventory for salamanders and snakes. Further work to document snake species at GEWA should include the use of coverboards as part of its sampling plan. (2) Elucidate park use by Diamond-backed Terrapins to provide a better understanding of the abundance, distribution, and habitat use of this rare species. (3) Areas of the park where there tend to be high concentrations of Box Turtles should be evaluated before opening them to recreational activities. (4) The public should not be allowed to release any animals that have been in captivity, and park management should educate park visitors on this issue. (5) Specific habitats that should be monitored on a regular basis at GEWA for the occurrence and persistence of amphibians and reptiles include tidal marshes, hardwood forests, and vernal pools. (6) Educational materials should be developed on the ecology, flora and fauna, and their interactions with human history at GEWA. (7) Park raccoon populations should be monitored, and population control measures implemented to protect all amphibians and reptiles, especially turtles and their nests. (8) Develop a comprehensive natural habitat management plan to conserve amphibians and reptiles at GEWA. (9) View long-term habitat management at GEWA within the context of the landscape matrix in and around the park.

Acknowledgments

Todd Georgel, Will Brown, and Kyle Walters assisted in the field. I thank Resource Manager Rijk Morawe for providing the collection permit, pertinent maps, some descriptive text of the park, and a variety of other forms of support for this project. I thank Beth Johnson, Sara Stevens, and John Karish and the National Park Service for providing the funding for this project.

Introduction

Over the past decade, the National Park Service has been working to establish what is now called the Inventory and Monitoring Program (I&M Program). The principal and simplified functions of this program are to gather existing as well as new information about the natural resources in the parks and to make that information easily available at different levels to park resource managers, the scientific community, and the public. Although some of the national parks in the United States have conducted field research on their existing flora and fauna (e.g., Braswell 1988; Mitchell and Anderson 1994; Hobson 1997, 1998; Forester 2000), many parks have never completed baseline species inventories. Where information exists, it is often incomplete and inaccurate including species outside of their native range (Mitchell 2000b). For park managers to effectively maintain the biological diversity and ecological health of their parks, they must have a basic knowledge of what natural resources exist in parks, as well as an understanding of those factors that may threaten them. One of the first goals of the I&M Program has been to establish baseline biological inventories for vascular plant and vertebrate species in order to provide reliable species lists, a fundamental tool for management.

Beyond developing a documented species list, being able to associate species and their habitats within the parks is critical to planning and development of an effective land management strategy. Resource managers need credible information on species and habitat requirements to develop effective policies, guidelines and management recommendations. Inventories that include locality, species richness, and population information will provide a valuable spatial database for managers to use for a variety of habitat-specific or site-specific management needs.

This report includes the results of a baseline amphibian and reptile inventory conducted at George Washington Birthplace National Monument (GEWA) in 2002. The George Washington Birthplace National Monument (GEWA) is located on the Northern Neck of rural and tidal Virginia about 45 miles east of Fredericksburg on highway 3 and about 80 miles south of Washington, D.C. in Westmoreland County.

The park is fairly flat, typical of the Coastal Plain, and is comprised of about 551 acres of lands bounded by the Potomac on the north, Pope's Creek estuary in the east and south and private land to the south and west. Salinity of Pope's Creek and other brackish water marshes within the park can be as much as 60% seawater. Habitats include about 280 acres of open grasslands (pasture and mowed), 220 acres of forests (heavily wooded and steep ravines with mixed deciduous hardwoods including large mature poplars, oaks and hickories; pine and red cedar forests), 25 acres of freshwater and brackish marshes and estuaries, 18 acres of memorial cultural landscapes, 5 acres of Potomac River beaches and dune habitats, and 3 acres of developed lands.

The biological resources of GEWA include a variety of animals and plants, including 50 birds, 34 fish, 23 mammals, and 513 vascular plants (National Park Service Biodiversity Database 2008). Prior to this study, 12 amphibians and 18 reptiles had been documented by Eckerlin, 1991. According to studies by the Virginia Department of Conservation and Recreation, Division of Natural Heritage, GEWA has 29 rare, threatened, and endangered species, including the bald eagle (*Haliaeetus leucocephalus*). Inventory reports indicate the importance of parklands and areas adjacent to the park. For more information, see the park's website at www.nps.gov/gewa/nature.

A search of the literature and museum specimen records for George Washington Birthplace National Monument confirmed the lack of information on amphibian and reptile species occurrence in the park. No museum records were found in the Smithsonian Institution [NMNH]) or other museums. The only published literature on the amphibians and reptiles of GEWA is Eckerlin (1991). Based on known distributions (Mitchell and Reay, 1999), 24 amphibian species and 28 reptile species could potentially occur at GEWA (Appendix A).

The GEWA herpetological inventory was conducted from 21 February to 1 October 2002 and from 22 March to 5 August 2003 (Appendix B). The project objectives were to 1) document 90% of the amphibians and reptiles at GEWA, 2) describe their associated habitats, and 3) provide park staff with conservation and management recommendations.

Study Area and Habitats

The inventory of amphibians and reptiles at GEWA was conducted at all accessible portions of the Park. George Washington Birthplace National Monument consists of one main geographic unit. A map of the locations where all amphibians and reptiles were inventoried is shown in Figure 1.

Nine habitat types were described by field crews as being used by amphibians and reptiles in GEWA[1]. Common and scientific names of the flora follow Radford et al. (1968). The habitat and microhabitat (location where animal was first sighted, e.g., under log, along pool margin, moving in open) was noted for each capture and observation.

Beach

Open sandy margins of land characteristic of the zone between dunes or terrestrial habitat and open water in river systems. There is no overstory, but tree species may occur along the beach border including: black locust (*Robinia pseudo-acacia*), sweetgum (*Liquidambar styraciflua*), loblolly pine (*Pinus taeda*), and persimmon (*Diospyros virginiana*). Shrubs include wax myrtle (*Myrica cerifera*), fetter-bush (*Pieris floribunda*), and blackberry (*Rubus* sp.), herbaceous plants include grasses, St. John's wort (*Hypericum* sp.), and thoroughwort (*Eupatorium* sp.). Vines include common greenbrier (*Smilax rotundifolia*) and trumpet vine (*Campsis radicans*).

Grasslands

Open fields dominated by grasses that are mowed on a regular to irregular basis or other land uses that have removed the forest canopy and created small patches of grass habitat. These areas include mixed grasses: Bermuda grass (*Cynodon dactylon*), velvet grass (*Holcus lanatus*), sweet vernal grass (*Anthoxanthum odoratum*), and broomsedge (*Andropogon virginicus*) and herbs, including dog fennel (*Anthemis* sp.), St. John's wort, wood sorrel (*Oxalis* sp.), and dandelion (*Taraxacum officinale*).

Marsh

Freshwater marshes that occur at the edges of impounds or along river courses. Most of the marshes at GEWA are floodplains in areas that receive tidal influence from the Potomac River. They are dominated by cattail (*Typha* sp.) with some cord grass (*Spartina* sp.). The edges of the floodplains are mostly composed of wax myrtle (*Myrica cerifera*) and common greenbrier shrubs. Overstory trees along the margins include loblolly pine (*Pinus taeda*), oaks (*Quercus alba, Quercus stellata, Quercus velutina*), tulip poplar (*Liriodendron tulipifera*), and willow (*Salix* sp.). The marshes sampled in this study all received tidal influence and are considered brackish.

---

[1] It is recommended that sampling location coordinates be cross-referenced with future vegetation maps to standardize habitat type nomenclature.

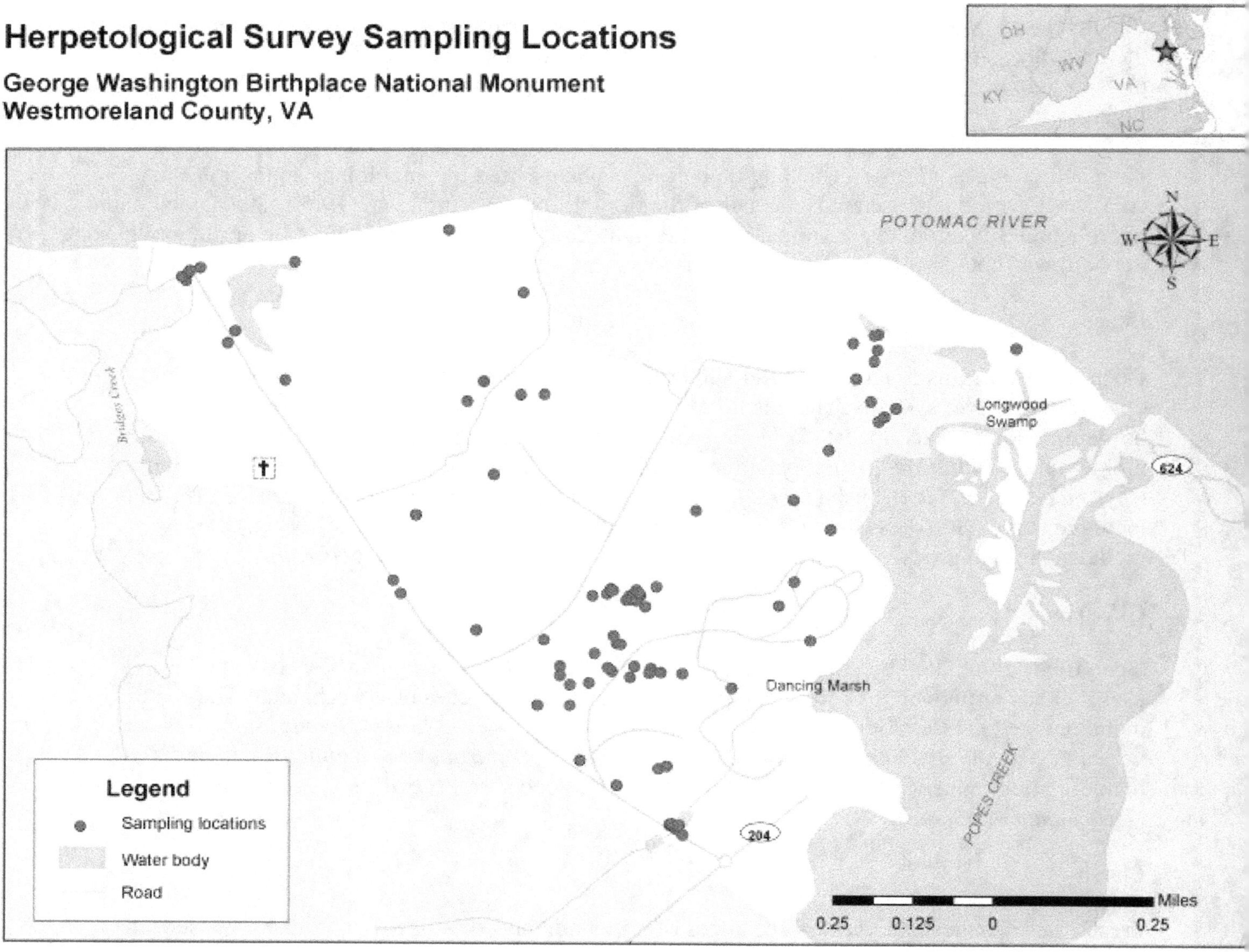

Herpetological Survey Sampling Locations
George Washington Birthplace National Monument
Westmoreland County, VA
OH
WV
KY
VA
NC
POTOMAC RIVER
N
W
E
S
Bridges Creek
Longwood Swamp
624
Dancing Marsh
POPES CREEK
204
Legend
Sampling locations
Water body
Road
Miles
0.25 0.125 0 0.25

Figure 1. Map showing observation and capture locations for amphibians and reptiles in George Washington Birthplace National Monument

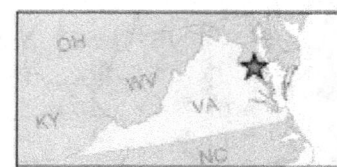

Mixed hardwoods and pine

Common wooded habitat at GEWA, consisting of loblolly pine, Virginia pine (*Pinus virginiana*), and hardwoods (oaks, sweet gum, tulip poplar). Understory trees include American holly (*Ilex opaca*), dogwood (*Cornus florida*), and some red maple (*Acer rubrum*) and ironwood (*Carpinus caroliniana*). Vines include trumpet creeper and common greenbrier, with an herbaceous layer of Pennsylvania smartweed (*Persicaria pennsylvanicum*) and grasses (*Panicum* sp.). Downed-woody debris varies throughout this habitat type.

Mixed hardwoods

Hardwood forests at GEWA lack a clear dominant overstory species, and include oaks, tulip poplar, red maple, beech (*Fagus grandifolia*), and blackgum (*Nyssa sylvatica*). The understory consists primarily of American holly, dogwood, blueberries (*Vaccinium* sp.) and huckleberries (*Gaylussacia* spp.) and saplings of overstory trees. The herbaceous layer is generally sparse, consisting of partridge berry (*Mitchella repens*), Pennsylvania smartweed (*Persicaria pennsylvanicum*), grasses, Christmas fern (*Polystichum acrostichoides*), cut-leafed grape fern (*Botrychium dissectum*), and seedlings of hardwoods and occasionally loblolly pine. Downed woody debris is a common feature on the forest floor. Several vernal pools (natural depressions in the landscape that hold water for varying times during the year, usually winter to summer) occur in this habitat type, varying in hydrology from short hydroperiods (weeks) to long hydroperiods (> 6 months) but usually drying out by the end of summer.

Mixed pine

Loblolly pine is the most common species, with other areas composed of Virginia pine. In some areas hardwood trees (red maple, sweet gum) are scattered among the pines, usually as understory trees. Herbs are sparse and include Pennsylvania smartweed, partridge berry (*Mitchella repens*); vines include poison ivy (*Rhus radicans*) and common greenbrier. Downed woody debris is less common than in the hardwood sites.

Impoundments

The primary impoundment at GEWA is a small pond on the southwest portion of the park. This pond is surrounded by mowed grasses with several large oak trees above the basin on the rim.

Swamp

Swamp habitat consists of shallow wetlands with woody vegetation, including red maple, bald cypress (*Taxodium distichum*), loblolly pine (*Pinus taeda*), and black willow (*Salix nigra*). The understory is sparse and usually consists of red maple and other soft hardwoods, and shrubs such as fetterbush. Grasses include saw grass (*Cladium jamaicense*), grasses (*Panicum* sp.), reeds (*Juncus* sp.), and broomsedge (*Andropogon* sp.).

Stream

We found no freshwater streams with seepages in GEWA.

Methods

Expected Species List Development

A list of species expected to occur at GEWA was developed based on the one scientific paper (Eckerlin 1991) and literature on Virginia amphibians and reptiles, especially the state amphibian and reptile atlas (Mitchell and Reay, 1999). The final expected species list is composed of 24 species of amphibians and 28 species of reptiles (Appendix A).

Sampling

Field survey work was conducted during amphibian and reptile activity seasons (late winter through October) in 2002 and 2003. The field schedule is outlined in detail in Appendix B.

A variety of sampling techniques were used to conduct the inventory at GEWA and are described in more detail for amphibians by Heyer et al. (1994) and Mitchell (2000a), and for reptiles by Jones (1986), Mitchell (1994), and Blomberg and Shine (1996). The protocols may vary when applied to monitoring (Heyer et al. 1994).

Visual Encounter Survey (VES)

Unstructured searches of selected habitats and microhabitats conducted by an experienced field herpetologist when the probability of encounter is high (appropriate weather and season for the targeted species). VES is sometimes referred to as haphazard or random searching; random searches, however, are seldom random, as an experienced herpetologist will preferentially search microhabitats that may yield results. A VES is conducted by walking in an unstructured manner through a selected habitat type, observing active amphibians and reptiles, as well as turning logs and other surface objects to uncover animals. Binoculars are used for searching water surfaces, logs, margins of wetlands, and basking places for frogs, lizards, snakes, and turtles. VES conducted as part of this inventory were not time-constrained.

Audio Survey

Detection of a frog species by its species-specific vocalization. Audio surveys were conducted during the day and also by night by listening for frog vocalizations at sites near roads. Audio surveys conducted as part of this inventory were not time-constrained.

Road Survey

Collection of either live or dead amphibians or reptiles on roads driven by day or night. Night time road surveys were primarily used during this inventory.

Dipnet Survey

Amphibian species detection through sampling with dipnets in aquatic microhabitats. The dipnets used in this inventory were D-ring aquatic nets with a fine mesh bag (Wards Biological Supply Co., Rochester, NY).

Minnow Trap Survey

Unbaited standard GEE minnow traps (Memphis Net and Twine, Memphis, TN) were set in shallow water with the upper 5-10 cm above the water surface to prevent drowning of air-breathing animals. Funnel openings were enlarged to 25-30 mm to increase capture success of adult frogs and semi-aquatic snakes. Wetlands were sampled for one day.

Turtle Trap Surveys

Standard turtle hoop traps (Memphis Net and Twine, Memphis, TN) were set in wetlands one day and removed the next. Traps used were (1) single funnel opening with nylon mesh on three 30 inch diameter steel hoops (nylon turtle nets) and (2) single funnel opening with nylon mesh on four 20 inch diameter fiberglass hoops (mini-hoop nets for catfish). Each trap was set with two poles on either side (opposite sides of the funnel opening). Each pole had an "L" hook imbedded at each end to hook into the terminal hoops; this extended the trap to its maximum length, ensured that the funnel opening was outstretched, and allowed easy setting in water. Traps were baited with a can of sardines in soybean oil; several holes were punched in the top of the can to allow the oil to dissipate the smell but prevented the turtles from eating the bait. Traps were set so that a portion was above the water surface to prevent the turtles from drowning.

Animal Measurements

All captured animals were handled in accordance with VA Department of Game and Inland Fisheries and National guidelines. No animals were harmed in the process, each being released at the site of capture.

All amphibian and reptiles captured were identified to species. Common and scientific names for amphibians and reptiles follow Crother (2000). Most animals were measured, weighed and gender determined. All measurements were recorded in millimeters and weights in grams. Body and tail measurements of amphibians were taken using plastic rulers, metric tapes and calipers. Weights were taken with Pesola® scales and Ohaus® Scout electronic field balances (Forestry Suppliers, Inc.). Animals seen or heard in the field but not captured were included in the database simply as observations (= present).

Frogs

Snout-Vent Length (SVL) was measured from the tip of the snout to the cloacal opening while the body was maintained in a straight line (i.e., making sure the sacral hump was flat).

Salamanders

SVL was taken from the tip of the snout to the posterior margin of the vent. Tail length was measured from the posterior vent margin to the tip of the tail when the tail was original and complete (not broken). For tails that were broken or had regenerated portions, the original tail portion was measured plus the length of the regenerated portion (resulting in numbers such as 19+21).

Lizards

SVL was taken from the tip of the snout to the posterior margin of the vent (anal plate). Tail length was taken from the posterior margin of the anal plate to the tip of the tail when the tail was original and complete (not broken). When tails were broken or had regenerated portions, then the original tail was measured plus the length of the regenerated portion (resulting in numbers such as 32+26).

Snakes

SVL was taken from the tip of the snout to the posterior margin of the anal plate with a metric tape, following the body curves. Tail length was taken from the posterior margin of the anal plate to the tip of the tail. Broken tails were simply noted, as these animals do not regenerate their tails like salamanders and lizards. Snakes were weighed in cloth or plastic bags; subtracting the weight of the bag to obtain the snake's weight.

Turtles

Carapace length (CL) and plastron lengths (PL) were taken with calipers (dial and tree) as straight-line measurements from the anterior-most point to the posterior-most point on the shell. The bar on the calipers was always parallel to the turtle's vertebral column.

Eastern Painted Turtles (*Chrysemys picta picta*) caught at GEWA were marked using a standard additive 1-2-4-7 code (Mitchell 1988) to assign unique numbers to the marginal scutes (Appendix C).

Location Data

Location data for George Washington Birthplace National Monument was collected using Magellan 310 and 315 hand-held GPS units [UTM (meters); Zone 18; NAD83]. Location information was recorded where an individual animal was caught or observed. When a defined terrestrial habitat area was searched, such as a field, a coordinate was taken at the center[2]. For wetlands, (e.g., pond, vernal pools) coordinates were taken where minnow traps or turtle traps were set, resulting in a single coordinate at one point along the margin. Search area boundaries changed once a new habitat type was encountered.

Photo Vouchers

Photographs were taken of the first individual of each species captured using a Nikon 6006 SLR with macro lens, and Fuji chrome Provia 100F slide film; slides were scanned at 300 dpi with a HP Scan jet 5370C slide scanner. Digital pictures were taken using a Nikon Coolpix 775 digital camera, set at 1600x1200 pixels (Normal). A list of photo vouchers by number and species name is provided in Appendix D.

---

[2] Terrestrial or aquatic amphibians and reptiles may move considerable distances through the habitat during daily or seasonal activities. Thus, single coordinates for areas locations was deemed appropriate, as long as the habitat was uniform.

Results

Inventory Results

Thirteen species of frogs, eleven species of salamanders, seven species of turtles, six species of lizards, and 15 species of snakes were expected to occur in GEWA based on available habitat types and known species distribution patterns (Eckerlin, 1991; Mitchell 1994; Mitchell and Reay 1999) (Table 1 and Appendix A). The current inventory documented 28 species of amphibians and reptiles. These include 8 frogs, representing 62% of the frog species expected to occur in the park, four salamanders, 36% of the expected salamander species, seven turtles representing 100% of the turtle species expected to occur in the park, three lizards, 50% of the species expected to occur, and six snakes, 40% of the snake species expected to occur. Total capture success was 50% for amphibians and 57% for reptiles.

A total of 341 individual animals were captured or observed during this inventory, including 232 amphibians (150 frogs, 82 salamanders) and 109 reptiles (81 turtles, 9 lizards, 19 snakes). Totals include all individual adults, frog tadpoles, and salamander larvae captured or observed. Pond-breeding frogs (*Rana catesbeiana, Rana clamitans melanota, Rana sphenocephala utricularia*) numerically dominated the frog fauna. The most abundant treefrog encountered was the Spring Peeper (*Pseudacris crucifer crucifer*). The salamander fauna consisted mostly of pond and pool-breeding species such as the ambystomatids (*Ambystoma maculatum* and *Ambystoma opacum*), newts (*Notophthalmus viridescens*). Neither of the two species of terrestrial salamanders (*Plethodon cylindraceus* and *Plethodon cinereus*) was encountered. Painted Turtles (*Chrysemys picta picta*) were the most numerous turtles found at GEWA, followed by Eastern Box Turtles (*Terrapene carolina carolina*). The snake fauna was the most difficult to sample. They tend to be secretive and that combined with the drought conditions that occurred during this inventory made them difficult to detect (see Discussion). In GEWA, Worm Snakes (*Carphophis amoenus amoenus)* were the most dominant species found in hardwood forests in the park, and Black Racers (*Coluber constrictor constrictor*) were the most common snake found in open areas.

No state or federally threatened species were found during this inventory. We found one fresh nest of the Diamond-backed Terrapin (*Malaclemys terrapin terrapin*) on the beach of the Potomac River.

Table 1. Checklist of the amphibians and reptiles of George Washington Birthplace National Monument, Virginia, documented during herpetological inventories conducted in 2002 and 2003.

Scientific name	Common name	Expected[a]	Eckerlin 1991[b]	Observed 2002[c]	Documented List[d]
Frogs					
Acris crepitans crepitans	Northern Cricket Frog	X	X	X	X
Bufo americanus americanus	American Toad	X	X		X
Bufo fowleri	Fowler's Toad	X	X	X	X
Gastrophryne carolinensis	Eastern Narrow-mouthed Toad	X			
Hyla chrysoscelis	Cope's Gray Treefrog	X	X	X	X
Hyla cinerea	Green Treefrog	X	X	X	X
Pseudacris crucifer crucifer	Northern Spring Peeper	X	X	X	X
Pseudacris feriarum	Upland Chorus Frog	X			
Rana catesbeiana	American Bullfrog	X	X	X	X
Rana clamitans melanota	Northern Green Frog	X	X	X	X
Rana palusriis	Pickerel Frog	X			
Rana sphenocephala utricularia	Southern Leopard Frog	X	X	X	X
Scaphiopus holbrookii	Eastern Spadefoot	X			
	Total	13	9	8	9
Salamanders					
Ambystoma maculatum	Spotted Salamander	X	X	X	X
Ambystoma opacum	Marbled Salamander	X	X	X	X
Desmognathus fuscus	Northern Dusky Salamander	X			
Eurycea cirrigera	Southern Two-lined Salamander	X			
Eurycea guttolineata	Three-lined Salamander	X			
Hemidactylium scutatum	Four-toed Salamander	X		X	X
Notophthalmus viridescens viridescens	Red-spotted Newt	X		X	X
Plethodon cinereus	Red-backed Salamander	X	X		X
Plethodon cylindraceus	White-spotted Slimy Salamander	X			
Pseudotriton montanus montanus	Mud Salamander	X			
Pseudotriton ruber ruber	Northern Red Salamander	X			
	Total	11	3	4	5

Table 1. Checklist of the amphibians and reptiles of George Washington Birthplace National Monument, Virginia, documented during herpetological inventories conducted in 2002 and 2003 (continued).

Scientific name	Common name	Expected[a]	Eckerlin 1991[b]	Observed 2002[c]	Documented List[d]
Turtles					
Chelydra serpentina serpentina	Common Snapping Turtle	X	X	X	X
Chrysemys picta picta	Eastern Painted Turtle	X	X	X	X
Kinosternon subrubrum subrubrum	Eastern Mud Turtle	X	X	X	X
Malaclemys terrapin terrapin	Northern Diamond-backed Terrapin	X	X	X	X
Pseudemys rubriventris	Red-bellied Cooter	X	X	X	X
Sternotherus odoratus	Eastern Musk Turtle	X		X	X
Terrapene carolina carolina	Eastern Box Turtle	X	X	X	X
	Total	7	6	7	7
Lizards					
Cnemidophorus sexlineatus sexlineatus	Six-lined Racerunner	X	X	X	X
Eumeces fasciatus	Five-lined Skink	X	X	X	X
Eumeces inexpectatus	Southeastern Five-lined Skink	X	X		X
Eumeces laticeps	Broad-headed Skink	X			
Sceloporus undulatus hyacinthinus	Fence Lizard	X	X		X
Scincella lateralis	Ground Skink	X	X	X	X
	Total	6	5	3	5
Snakes					
Agkistrodon contortrix mokasen	Northern Copperhead	X			
Carphophis amoenus amoenus	Eastern Worm Snake	X	X	X	X
Coluber constrictor constrictor	Northern Black Racer	X		X	X
Diadophis punctatus edwardsii	Northern Ring-necked Snake	X		X	X
Elaphe obsoleta obsoleta	Black Ratsnake	X	X	X	X
Heterodon platirhinos	Eastern Hog-nosed Snake	X			
Lampropeltis calligaster rhombomaculata	Mole Kingsnake	X			

Table 1. Checklist of the amphibians and reptiles of George Washington Birthplace National Monument, Virginia, and its subunits, documented during herpetological inventories conducted in 2002 and 2003 (continued).

Scientific name	Common name	Expected[a]	Eckerlin 1991[b]	Observed 2002[c]	Documented List[d]
Snakes (continued)					
Lampropeltis getula getula	Eastern Kingsnake	X	X		X
Nerodia sipedon sipedon	Northern Watersnake	X	X	X	X
Opheodrys aestivus	Rough Greensnake	X	X		X
Storeria dekayi dekayi	Northern Brownsnake	X		X	X
Storeria occipitomaculata occipitomaculata	Red-bellied Snake	X			
Thamnophis sauritus sauritus	Northern Ribbonsnake	X	X		X
Thamnophis sirtalis sirtalis	Eastern Gartersnake	X	X		X
Virginia valeriae valeriae	Smooth Earthsnake	X			
	Table	15	7	6	10

[a] Expected-species that should occur in GEWA given distribution patterns and available habitat from Mitchell and Reay (1999).
[b] Eckerlin, 1991-species observed in this study.
[c] Observed-species observed or captured during the 2002 and 2003 inventory.
[d] Documented-total of the columns for Eckerlin (1991) and the observations made during this study

14

Sampling Success

Table 2 provides the number of individuals of each species documented at GEWA in relation to the sampling methods used. More species were detected using the Visual Encounter Survey protocol (VES) than any other protocol (26 of the 28 species encountered in 2002 and 2003). Audio surveys resulted in one frog species not encountered using VES (*Hyla chrysoscelis*). VES and road surveys revealed one frog species not detected by the audio protocol (*Bufo fowleri*). Except for lizards and snakes, multiple protocols were necessary to encounter the species of each taxonomic group. Lizards and snakes were documented only by the VES protocol.

Species-Habitat Associations

Distribution of capture and observation records for amphibians and reptiles among nine habitat types reveal that no species is a habitat specialist at GEWA (Table 3). Those with three or more records confined to a single habitat type include *Acris crepitans crepitans* in impoundments, *Pseudacris crucifer crucifer* in marshes and impoundments, *Rana catesbeiana* in mixed hardwoods and pine, impoundments and swamps, *Rana clamitans melanota* in mixed hardwood pine and impoundments, *Rana sphenocephala ultrularia* in marshes, mixed hardwoods and impoundments, *Ambystoma maculatum* in mixed hardwood pine and mixed hardwoods, *Ambystoma opacum* in mixed hardwoods, *Notophthalmus viridescens viridescens* in impoundments and swamps, *Chelydra serpentina serpentina*, *Chrysemys picta picta*, and *Pseudemys rubriventris* in impoundments, *Terrapene carolina carolina* in mixed hardwoods and pine, *Carphophis amoenus amoenus* in mixed hardwoods, and *Coluber constrictor constrictor* in mixed hardwoods and pine. Of all nine habitat types, the three that support the most species of amphibians and reptiles on GEWA, based on these data, are mixed hardwoods and pine (16 species), mixed hardwoods (15 species), and impoundments (13 species).

Table 2. Number of individuals of each herpetological species documented by sampling method at George Washington Birthplace National Monument during 2002 and 2003 inventories.

	Sampling Method					
	Audio Survey	Dipnet Survey	Minnow Traps	Turtle Traps	Road Survey	Visual Encounter Survey
Frogs						
Acris crepitans crepitans	3	2				3
Bufo fowleri					4	15
Hyla chrysoscelis	2					
Hyla cinerea	1					2
Pseudacris crucifer crucifer	9					19
Rana catesbeiana	2	3	13			3
Rana clamitans melanota	5	4	1		1	13
Rana sphenocephala utricularia	6	1	23		1	14
Salamanders						
Ambystoma maculatum		31				23
Ambystoma opacum		8				8
Hemidactylium scutatum						1
Notophthalmus viridescens viridescens		4	5			2
Turtles						
Chelydra serpentine serpentina				1		6
Chrysemys picta picta				35		9
Kinosternon subrubrum subrubrum						2
Malaclemys terrapin terrapin						1
Pseudemys rubriventris						5
Sternotherus odoratus				2		
Terrapene carolina carolina						20
Lizards						
Cnemidophorus sexlineatus sexlineatus						3
Eumeces fasciatus						5
Scincella lateralis						1
Snakes						
Carphophis amoenus amoenus						10
Coluber constrictor constrictor						4
Diadophis punctatus edwardsii						1
Elaphe obsoleta obsoleta						1
Nerodia sipedon sipedon						2
Storeria dekayi dekayi						1
Total Individuals encountered	28	53	42	38	6	174
Total Species encountered	7	7	4	3	3	26

Table 3. Numbers of individual amphibian and reptiles captured or observed among nine habitat types at George Washington Birthplace National Monument, Virginia, during 2002 and 2003.

	Habitat Type*								
	BEA	GRA	MAR	MHP	MHW	MPI	IMP	SWA	STR
Frogs									
Acris crepitans crepitans			2	2	1		3		
Bufo fowleri		18		1	1				
Hyla chrysoscelis				1	1				
Hyla cinerea			1				1		
Pseudacris crucifer crucifer		1	10	3	1		5		
Rana catesbeiana			1	6			8	6	
Rana clamitans melanota			2	6	1		3		
Rana sphenocephala utricularia			3	1	7		31		
Salamanders									
Ambystoma maculatum				8	38				
Ambystoma opacum				2	14				
Hemidactylium scutatum				1					
Notophthalmus viridescens viridescens					1		5	5	
Turtles									
Chelydra serpentine serpentina	1		2	1			3		
Chrysemys picta picta							44		
Kinosternon subrubrum subrubrum		1			1				
Malaclemys terrapin terrapin	1								
Pseudemys rubriventris							5		
Sternotherus odoratus							2		
Terrapene carolina carolina				8		2			
Lizards									
Cnemidophorus sexlineatus sexlineatus	1	2							
Eumeces fasciatus		2		1	2				
Scincella lateralis					1				
Snakes									
Carphophis amoenus amoenus					10				
Coluber constrictor constrictor				3	1		1		
Diadophis punctatus edwardsii				1					
Elaphe obsoleta obsoleta					1				
Nerodia sipedon sipedon							2		
Storeria dekayi dekayi				1					
Total Individuals	3	24	21	46	81	2	113	11	0
Total Species	3	5	7	16	15	1	13	2	0

*Abbreviations: BEA = Beach, GRA = Grasslands, MAR = Marsh, MHP = Mixed hardwood and pine, MHW = Mixed hardwoods, MPI = Mixed pine, IMP = Impoundments, SWA = Swamp, STR = Stream

Discussion

Inventory

Amphibians and reptiles are seasonal animals whose activity patterns respond to changes in climate, temperature, and precipitation. Thus, a complete inventory of amphibians and reptiles can be a challenge during short-term surveys, especially given the climatic conditions that occurred during the primary study period in 2002. Precipitation, as recorded at Colonial Beach, Westmoreland County and Warsaw, Richmond County, Virginia, was below average most months (NOAA Climatological Summary, Asheville, NC). Normal rainfall occurred only in April 2002. Rainfall in all other months in which amphibians and reptiles were active was well below the 30-year average. These conditions likely influenced the encounter probability and capture success of amphibian and reptile species at GEWA during the primary phase of this inventory. In particular, because the winter of 2001-2002 was abnormally dry; water tables were not replenished and surface depression wetlands not filled, leaving many breeding sites unavailable to amphibians and reptiles in 2002. Rainfall in 2003 was generally normal to above normal except in January when precipitation total was 1.8 inches below normal.

Notwithstanding the climatic limitations, the species encountered during this survey represent a robust list for all groups of amphibians and reptiles, especially when the results from Eckerlin (1991) and the current inventory are combined. Inventory success for 2002 alone, based upon the expected species list for GEWA, ranged from 36% to 100%. Most of the frog species were found during both inventories, with Eckerlin (1991) finding only one species not documented during this survey (*Bufo americanus*).

The low sighting and capture rate for salamanders (36%) is a result of no freshwater springs and/or seeps existing at GEWA. Five species usually occur in association with these wetland types, (*Desmognathus fuscus, Eurycea cirrigera, Eurycea guttolineata, Pseudotriton montanus montanus, and Pseudotriton ruber ruber*). Eckerlin (1991) found one species of salamander not documented during this survey, the Red-backed Salamander (*Plethodon cinereus*). On the other hand, two salamander species were documented during this survey, not found by Eckerlin in 1991: Four-toed Salamander (*Hemidactylium scutatum*) and Red-spotted Newt (*Notophthalmus viridescens viridescens*).

Fifty percent of the expected lizard species were captured during this survey. Fence Lizards (*Sceloporus undulatus hyacinthinus*) were not documented in the Park, usually a conspicuous species. One species (*Eumeces laticeps*) may not occur at GEWA, and the other species of lizards not encountered (Table 1) may have been due to the extreme dry conditions during the survey.

All of the expected species of turtles were documented during this survey. One turtle captured, the Stinkpot (*Sternotherus odoratus*), was not recorded by Eckerlin.

Only six of the 15 species of snakes expected to occur at GEWA were documented during the 2002 inventory. Eckerlin (1991) found four species we did not find: Eastern Kingsnake

(*Lampropeltis getula getula*), Rough Greensnake (*Opheodrys aestivus*), Ribbonsnake (*Thamnophis sauritus*), and Eastern Gartersnake (*Thamnophis sirtalis sirtalis*). During this inventory, three additional species not recorded by Eckerlin were found: Black Racer (*Coluber constrictor constrictor*), Northern Ring-necked Snake (*Diadophis punctatus edwardsii*), and Northern Brownsnake (*Storeria dekayi dekayi*).

Snake species that were not encountered, but were expected to occur at GEWA include the Northern Copperhead (*Agkistrodon contortrix mokasen*), Eastern Hog-nosed Snake (*Heterodon platirhinos*), Mole Kingsnake (*Lampropeltis calligaster rhombomaculata*), Red-bellied Snake (*Storeria occipitomaculata*), and Smooth Earthsnake (*Virginia valeriae valeriae*). Additional trips and chance observations in favorable weather conditions would be required to add more snake species to the park's list. Many snakes are active for only short periods of time during favorable weather, usually warm and wet periods (Wright and Wright 1957; Gibbons and Semlitsch 1987), and few species of snakes move with sufficient frequency to be encountered when it is dry. Snakes in general can be especially hard to survey; many are secretive and occur in limited numbers (Gibbons et al. 1997). Leiden et al. (1999) demonstrated with multiple techniques that 66% of the total snake species expected were caught in the first 75 days of sampling, but that an additional 325 days of sampling would be required to collect 90% of the total number expected. Whiteman et al. (1995) and Gibbons et al. (1997) showed that it took over 22 years to discover one snake species on the Savannah River Site, an area that has been intensively studied for over 40 years.

Based on distribution patterns of amphibian and reptile species in Virginia (Mitchell 1994; Mitchell and Reay 1999), all of the species encountered during this survey were expected to occur in GEWA. The combined lists of Eckerlin (1991) and that from our 2002-2003 study resulted in a nearly complete inventory of the amphibians and reptiles in GEWA.

Sampling Method Efficiency

Because amphibians and reptiles are notoriously secretive animals, successful species documentation depends upon the use of multiple capture techniques in both wetland and terrestrial habitats (Corn and Bury 1990; Heyer et al. 1994; Ryan et al. 2002). Determining which method(s) are most effective depends on the goal of the inventory as well as the behaviors and habitats of target species expected to be encountered. VES often detects the greatest numbers of species, as was the case in this survey, detecting 26 of the 28 species encountered (Table 2). However, this survey method will not provide quantitative data useful for estimating population size or structure, habitat preferences, habitat use during different life stages or distribution. It is also important to note that VES is difficult to replicate in future efforts, as they lack rigor from a sampling and statistical perspective, and are essentially qualitative rather than quantitative. Thus, this method is only effective for documenting the occurrence of amphibian and reptile species, as for an inventory of GEWA.

The results of this survey also indicate that methods vary in their effectiveness at detecting different species, even those within the same taxonomic group such as frogs. Considering the diversity of amphibian and reptiles and the variability in their size, modes of reproduction, patterns of habitat use, degree of habitat specialization and life history, this is expected. To account for this, a generalized, multi-habitat inventory should always incorporate a number of different methods. Choice of methods will depend to a certain extent on the relative importance placed on detecting species presence versus generating quantitative estimates of abundance, population size and structure, and habitat comparisons, as well as what the potential species are. Based on the GEWA inventory, audio surveys, dipnet surveys, and minnow and turtle traps, when augmented by VES, were most effective for the generalized inventory of this park.

For frogs, the combination of audio surveys and VES proved to be the most effective documentation method. For turtles, the combination of trapping and VES was most effective although four species were observed only with the latter method. Use of minnow traps is an effective way to inventory salamander larvae and frog tadpoles. Minnow traps should always be considered when developing inventory plans. Other survey methods such as road surveys can be an effective technique for documenting snakes, turtles and frogs, although success depends greatly on weather and seasonal activity patterns. This method proved unreliable in GEWA.

One method that should be considered specifically for the documentation of snakes is coverboard surveys. The use of coverboards, quarter sheets of plywood, roofing tin, or other similar material laid out in selected areas on the ground, could have been used to potentially enhance snake capture success at GEWA. Coverboards were not used in this study as it was assumed that there would be logs and other surface cover objects available throughout the park for searching. Unfortunately there were fewer natural cover objects available than expected in areas that might have harbored small snakes. Other methods that could potentially be used to survey snakes include glueboards and drift fences with pitfall traps. However, glueboards can result in the death of animals so are not highly recommended. While drift fence and pitfall traps require a large effort to install and operate (Gibbons and Semlitsch 1981). The Virginia Department of Game and Inland Fisheries requires that pitfalls be checked at least every other day, a sampling intensity not supported by the budget for this particular inventory. In the future, additional work to document the snake fauna at GEWA should include the use of coverboards placed in selected habitats around the park.

Species-Habitat Associations

Protection of selected habitats could allow viable populations of native amphibians and reptiles to persist in GEWA. Amphibians and reptiles function in a landscape context (Semlitsch 2003), and a mix of habitat types is essential for their existence in the park. Long-term preservation of the amphibian and reptile populations at GEWA will require the management and maintenance of a variety of landscape types. Factors that may impact this mosaic should be identified and addressed in the park management plan. Habitats that support relatively unique assemblage of these vertebrates include hardwood forests, tidal marshes, the ice pond, and vernal pools.

The habitat classification used in the current study was based on general field descriptions and is indicative of the ecological conditions favorable to amphibians and reptiles (e.g., Wright and Wright 1957; Martof et al. 1980; Mitchell 1994; Conant and Collins 1998). These animals rely more on the environmental structure (shelter, temperature, relative humidity) provided by plant community environments rather than individual plant species composition (personal observations). Most amphibians and reptiles use multiple habitat types that are adjacent to one another during their daily and seasonal movements (e.g., Reinert 1993; Buhlmann 2001; Semlitsch 2003), and may travel one or more kilometers (e.g., Gregory et al. 1987; Semlitsch

1998; Semlitsch and Bodie 1998; Pauley et al. 2000). Some habitats may be used by species only during movements from one primary habitat to another and other species can move among several habitat types in a single day or season. Therefore a record in a single habitat type may only be a snapshot of habitat preference by a species. Only detailed studies of movements using radio-telemetry can reveal all the habitats selected in a given area (e.g., Reinert 1993; Carter et al. 1999).

Important components of the existing GEWA landscape necessary for maintaining amphibian and reptile species include: 1) the matrix or combination of freshwater vernal pools and hardwood forest habitats throughout the park. Both Spotted Salamanders and Marbled Salamanders (*Ambystoma* sp.) were predominately found in hardwood forests in the southwestern side of the park. This habitat contains several vernal pools that are essential breeding habitats for these salamander species. These predominately subterranean salamanders spend most of their lives in the forested areas surrounding the vernal pools in which they breed. The hardwood forests contain an underground tunnel matrix required by these salamanders that seldom create their own burrows. These species must have a combination of habitat types such as the vernal pools and surrounding hardwood forest, in order to meet their life history requirements. Loss of one of these habitat types will result in the loss of these species in the park. Appropriate corridors connecting hardwood forests and vernal pools are essential landscape features that greatly influence the viability of ambystomatid salamander populations in GEWA.

The amount of terrestrial habitat used by Spotted and Marbled salamanders (*Ambystoma* sp.) depends on the distances these species travel away from their breeding pool or pond. Averages from several studies has shown that at least 164.3 meters of terrestrial habitat is required around a breeding pool to protect 95% of an *Ambystoma* salamander population (Semlitsch 1998). Most amphibians move considerably further; for example, many frogs and salamanders have been documented to travel over a kilometer from their aquatic breeding sites (Pauley et al. 2000). Thus, effective ambystomatid conservation will require preserving several hundred meters of appropriate terrestrial habitat (specifically mature hardwood forests) around much of the breeding pools or ponds in the park. In the best of circumstances, preserving areas composed of terrestrial habitat with an imbedded complex of vernal pools is ideal.

Another important factor to consider in the conservation of amphibian species is their movement between breeding pools and ponds in order to maintain viable populations. Maintaining viable populations of amphibians in the park will require that these animals be able to disperse across habitats and among breeding areas, and that dispersal corridors be included in any species management plan. Recently discussed in the literature, habitat conservation strategies for amphibians must include the maintenance and preservation of a core habitat composed of breeding pools or ponds and the terrestrial habitat surrounding them (165 m average) surrounded by an additional buffer zone (Semlitsch and Jensen 2001).

Aquatic habitats (impoundments, swamps, and tidal marshes) support a diverse array of species, with many species using more than one of these habitats in GEWA. Ranid frogs and turtles were the dominant fauna found in the park's impoundments, while shallow-water breeders (e.g., hylid frogs) were the most common species found in the marshes.

This inventory only provides a snapshot of habitat types that amphibian and reptile species use at THST. No quantitative analysis can be done to rank the use of habitat types by species.
A complete picture of the existing landscape matrix must be considered when managing areas that support herpetological species. Although most of the herpetological species at THST were documented in Mixed Hardwood and Pine habitat (MHP) or Mixed-Hardwood habitat (MHW) (Table 3), the number and extent of the vernal pools within this MHP and MHW habitat must also be considered. MHP and MHW habitats devoid of vernal pools would most likely support a completely different assemblage of amphibian and reptile species than recorded during this inventory.

Threats to Amphibian and Reptile Populations

Effective amphibian and reptile management first requires threat identification. The threats to these vertebrates at GEWA include human disturbance or killing, mortality from vehicular traffic, boat traffic, the effects of herbicides and pesticides, subsidized predators, and habitat loss or alteration. Habitat loss is not considered a major threat at GEWA. Future plans for alteration of areas of park land that may include habitat loss should be reviewed thoroughly and losses prevented when possible.

Human Disturbance, Vehicles, and Recreational Activities

Removal of animals by humans for personal or the commercial pet trade constitutes an unknown threat level as there is no data to evaluate this impact. Garber and Burger (1995) found that opening an area to recreation resulted in the complete loss of a Wood Turtle (*Clemmys insculpta*) population, caused primarily by removal of turtles by humans and dogs. Humans pick up Box Turtles and will remove them or at least carry them to other locations in the park. This results in the loss of an important reproductive individual to the population. Areas of the park where there tend to be high concentrations of Box Turtles should be evaluated before opening them to recreational activities.

Rates of mortality on park roads and in the Potomac River that support boat traffic are unknown, but could be significant for some species. Knowing these rates and better understanding the seasonality of road mortalities in the park will help resource managers to better manage potential problem areas, and allow steps to minimize vehicular mortality on park roads.

Herbicide and Pesticide Effects on Amphibians

Ecotoxicology studies of herbicide and pesticide effects on amphibians have not been thorough and often use only a laboratory species not found in North America (McDiarmid and Mitchell 2000). Spraying herbicides and pesticides in and over terrestrial and wetland habitats could produce harmful results to amphibian populations, especially at the larval stage. The use of larvacides for mosquito control (West Nile virus) in wetlands such as vernal pools is also likely to be harmful to larval-staged amphibians. Decisions to use chemicals for natural resource management should thus be made with extreme caution, and larval populations monitored both prior to and post spraying of pesticides.

Box Turtles as Indicators of Ecosystem Health: Box turtles may be excellent indicators of ecosystem condition and health. During a recent Box turtle study, it was found that nearly all turtles captured in the Blacksburg, Virginia area, had high levels of organochlorine pesticide in their systems (Holladay et al. 2001). In addition, Holladay et al., 2001 and Brown et al., 2004 noted the development of aural (ear) abscesses as a result of vitamin A deficiency caused by organochlorine pesticide contamination. Organochlorine pesticides are used in agricultural applications in areas such as Blacksburg, VA, and such chemicals may be used in the area surrounding GEWA.

25

During this inventory at GEWA, no turtles with aural abscesses were found, suggesting that this may not currently be a problem at GEWA. Annual monitoring for aural abscesses on Box turtles in GEWA may help detect possible organochlorine pesticide contamination within the park.

Exotics and Subsidized Predators

Scavenging or predatory mammals usually exist at higher population densities in areas of high human use due to the existence of garbage, discarded food and structures as shelters. Raccoons, which are notorious for killing and eating turtle adults and eggs in nests, can dramatically decrease populations of these species. They also eat frogs and any other amphibian or reptile they can catch. Other animals that qualify as subsidized predators (Mitchell and Klemens 2000) include foxes, opossums, skunks, and crows. The introduced house cat (free-ranging and feral) is also included in this category because they kill large numbers of native animals (Mitchell and Beck 1992). Populations of raccoons and other subsidized predators, especially cats, are likely contributing to declines in some native species populations at GEWA. An evaluation of the size of the raccoon population in the park, as well as mapping their distribution in relation to park use activities, should be undertaken. Identification of primary turtle nesting sites and evaluation of nest loss to raccoons and other subsidized predators should also be conducted. Such information would allow informed management decisions about control of the raccoon population

Finally, captive-raised or captive-bred amphibians and reptiles should not be released at GEWA under any circumstances. The potential for disease introduction is growing and every effort should be made to avoid contamination from exotics. Captivity often induces stress and influences development of disease. The public should not be allowed to release any animals that have been in captivity, and park management should educate park visitors on this issue.

Habitat Management

Long-term habitat management at GEWA would benefit if management issues and potential construction impacts were viewed within the context of the park's landscape matrix as a whole. Any change to hardwood forests at GEWA, for example, may have consequences to Spotted Salamander and Box Turtle populations.

Specific habitats should be monitored at GEWA for the occurrence and persistence of amphibians and reptiles, including vernal pools, mature hardwoods, and tidal marshes and beach. Hardwood forest habitats are critical areas for some amphibians and reptiles. Forests with full to partial canopy and a well-defined forest floor with downed woody debris provide important microhabitat for several species, and should be maintained with the concept of "old growth" in mind.

A comprehensive natural habitat management plan for the conservation of native species and their habitats should be developed for GEWA. This is a unique area that has been the focus of many years of protection and research due to its human history. However, its natural history has received little to no attention. A habitat management plan for this historic site would ensure that this area is maintained in its natural conditions. The working/research committee for such a plan could include experts in all floral and faunal groups, as well as forest and wetland conservation biologists.

Additional Inventory Work

Additional species documentation work is needed for salamanders and snakes. Further work to document snake species at GEWA should include the use of coverboards as part of its sampling plan. Additional documentation to add to the overall amphibian and reptile species list for GEWA could be accomplished in three ways: (1) routine accumulation of digital photographs of road-kills, especially snakes, with appropriate documentation (date and location), (2) use of several coverboard arrays monitored periodically, and (3) use of natural history (animal) sighting cards filled out by knowledgeable visitors. Reinstatement of the latter program would result in a valuable source of information for natural resource management staff if accompanied by verifiable information such as a photograph. In addition, further herpetological work at GEWA could include methods for acquiring species abundance and detailed distribution information for all species documented during this inventory.

The Copperhead, the only venomous snake in the area, was not found during our survey or by Eckerlin (1991). Their low occurrence frequency and apparent spotty distribution on the Upper Peninsula suggest that education may be the only reasonable approach that could be used by park personnel to address their presence and this potential threat to humans.

Habitat Restricted Species

Most of the herpetological species found at GEWA are those that occur throughout the Upper Peninsula in eastern Virginia. Many of these species use a variety of habitats during daily movements, as well as seasonal movements to breeding pools and ponds. The exception is the Northern Diamond-backed Terrapin which requires estuarine habitat. Additional inventory work on each individual habitat type should be considered to better understand the abundance and distributions of amphibians and reptiles within them.

The occurrence of Diamond-backed Terrapins in the tidal marsh was not unexpected because this turtle has been observed in the Potomac River (Mitchell 1994; Mitchell and Reay 1999). This species has declined dramatically in the Chesapeake Bay and throughout much of its range in recent decades (Seigel and Gibbons 1995; Mitchell 1994). Although its population status at GEWA and in the Potomac River is unknown, Diamond-backed Terrapins are uniquely adapted to estuarine habitats, and indeed is the only truly estuarine reptile in the world. This species' discovery in the tidal marsh raises several questions of management concern, including mortality rates from boat propellers and the associated deterioration in environmental quality through pollutants. Management options could include education on this species, and limiting the number and speed of boats. Further inventory work to determine park use by this species would assist in their future management within the park.

Literature Cited

Blomberg, S., and R. Shine. 1996. Reptiles. Pages 218-226 *in* W.J. Sutherland, editor. Ecological Census Techniques, a Handbook. Cambridge University Press. Cambridge, UK.

Braswell, A. L. 1988. Preliminary report on a survey of the herpetofauna of Cape Hatteras National Seashore. Unpublished report submitted to the National Park Service. NC State Museum of Natural Sciences, Raleigh, NC. 13 pp.

Buhlmann, K. A. 2001. Terrestrial habitat use by aquatic turtles from a seasonally fluctuating wetland: implications for wetland conservation boundaries. Chelonian Conservation and Biology 4:115-127.

Carter, S. L., C. A. Haas, and J. C. Mitchell. 1999. Home range and habitat selection of bog turtles in southwestern Virginia. Journal of Wildlife Management 63:853-860.

Conant, R., and J. T. Collins. 1998. A Field Guide to Reptiles and Amphibians Eastern and Central North America. 3rd expanded edition. Peterson Field Guide Series. Houghton Mifflin Co. Boston, MA. 616 pp.

Corn, P. S., and R. B. Bury. 1990. Sampling methods for terrestrial amphibians and reptiles. US Department of Agriculture, Forest Service, General Technical Report PNW-GTR-256.

Crother, B. I. (committee chair). 2000. Scientific and standard English names of amphibians and reptiles of North America north of Mexico, with comments regarding confidence in our understanding. SSAR Herpetological Circular 29:1-82.

Dodd, C. K., Jr. 2001 North American Box Turtles, A Natural History. University of Oklahoma Press. Norman, OK. 231 pp.

Eckerlin, R. P. 1991. The Herpofauna of George Washington Birthplace National Monument, Virginia. Catesbeiana 11(1):11-17.

Forester, D. C. 2000. Amphibian inventory Chesapeake and Ohio Canal and National Historic Park. Unpublished report to the National Park Service. Washington, DC. 62 pp.

Garber, S. D., and J. Burger. 1995. A 20-year study documenting the relationship between turtle decline and human recreation. Ecological Applications 5:1151-1162.

Gibbons, J. W., and R. D. Semlitsch. 1981. Terrestrial drift fences with pitfall traps: an effective technique for quantitative sampling of animal populations. Brimleyana 7:1-16.

Gibbons, J. W., and R. D. Semlitsch. 1987. Activity patterns. Pp. 396-421 *In* R.A. Seigel, J.T. Collins, and S.S. Novak, editors. Snakes: Ecology and Evolutionary Biology. Macmillan Publishing Co. New York, NY.

Gibbons, J. W., V. J. Burke, J. E. Lovich, R. D. Semlitsch, T. D. Tuberville, J. R. Bodie, J. R. Greene, P. H. Niewiarowski, H. H. Whiteman, D. E. Scott, and others. 1997. Perceptions of species abundance, distribution, and diversity: lessons from four decades of sampling on a government-managed reserve. Environmental Management 21:259-268.

Gregory, P. T., J. M. Macartney, and K. W. Larsen. 1987. Spatial patterns and movements. Pages 366-395 *in* R. A. Seigel, J. T. Collins, and S. S. Novak, editors. Snakes: Ecology and Evolutionary Biology. Macmillan Publishing Co. New York, NY.

Heyer, W. R., M. A. Donnelly, R. W. McDiarmid, L. C. Hayek, and M. S. Foster. 1994. Measuring and Monitoring Biological Diversity, Standard Methods for Amphibians. Smithsonian Institution Press. Washington, DC. 364 pp.

Hobson, C. S. 1997. A natural heritage inventory of groundwater invertebrates within the Virginia portions of the George Washington Memorial Parkway including Great Falls Park. Natural Heritage Technical Report 97-9. Virginia Department of Conservation and Recreation, Division of Natural Heritage, Richmond. Unpublished report submitted to the National Park Service. 36 pp. + appendix.

Hobson, C. S. 1998. A natural heritage inventory of the Cheatham and Wormley Pond drainages, Colonial National Historical Park. Natural Heritage Technical Report 98-11. Virginia Department of Conservation and Recreation, Division of Natural Heritage. Richmond, VA. 42 pp. + appendices.

Holladay, S. D., J. C. Wolf, S. A. Smith, D. E. Jones, and J. L. Robertson. 2001. Aural abscesses in wild-caught box turtles (*Terrapene carolina*): possible role of organochlorine-induced hypervitaminosis A. Ecotoxicology and Environmental Safety 48:99-106.

Jones, K. B. 1986. Amphibians and reptiles. Pages 267-290 *in* A. Y. Cooperrider, R. J. Boyd, and H. R. Stuart, editors. Inventory and Monitoring of Wildlife Habitat. U.S. Dept. of Interior, Bureau of Land Management Service Center. Denver, CO.

Leiden, Y. A., M. E. Dorcas, and J. W. Gibbons. 1999. Herpetofaunal diversity in Coastal Plain communities of South Carolina. Journal of the Elisha Mitchell Scientific Society 115:270-280.

Martof, B. S., W. M. Palmer, J. R. Bailey, and J. R. Harrison, III. 1980. Amphibians and Reptiles of the Carolinas and Virginia. University of North Carolina Press. Chapel Hill, NC. 264 pp.

McDiarmid, R. W., and J. C. Mitchell. 2000. Diversity and distribution of amphibians and reptiles. Pages 15-69 *in* D. W. Sparling, G. Linder, and C. A. Bishop (eds.), Ecotoxicology of Amphibians and Reptiles. Society of Environmental Toxicology and Chemistry, SETAC Press, Pensacola, FL.

Mitchell, J. C. 1988. Population ecology and life histories of the freshwater turtles *Chrysemys picta* and *Sternotherus odoratus* in an urban lake. Herpetological Monographs 2:40-61.

Mitchell, J. C. 1994. The Reptiles of Virginia. Smithsonian Institution Press, Washington, DC. 352 pp.

Mitchell, J. C. 2000a. Amphibian Monitoring Methods & Field Guide. Smithsonian National Zoological Park, Conservation Research Center, Front Royal, VA. 56 pp.

Mitchell, J. C. 2000b. Amphibians and reptiles of the National Capital Parks: Review of existing information and inventory methods. Unpublished report to the National Park Service, Washington, DC. 50 pp.

Mitchell, J. C., and J. M. Anderson. 1994. Amphibians and Reptiles of Assateague and Chincoteague Islands. Virginia Museum of Natural History, Martinsville, VA. 120 pp.

Mitchell, J. C., and R. A. Beck. 1992. Free-ranging domestic cat predation on native vertebrates in rural and urban Virginia. Virginia Journal of Science 43:197-207.

Mitchell, J. C., and M. W. Klemens. 2000. Primary and secondary effects of habitat alteration. Pages 5-32 inn M. W. Klemens, editor. Turtle Conservation. Smithsonian Institution Press, Washington, D.C.

Mitchell, J. C. and K. K. Reay. 1999. Atlas of Amphibians and Reptiles in Virginia. Special Publication Number 1, Department of Game and Inland Fisheries, Richmond, VA. 122 pp.

The National Park Service Biodiversity Database. Secure online version. https://science1.nature.nps.gov/npspecies/web/main/start (certified organisms; accessed March 10, 2008)

Pauley, T. K., J. C. Mitchell, R. R. Buech, and J. J. Moriarty. 2000. Ecology and management of riparian habitats for amphibians and reptiles. Pp. 169-192 *in* E. S. Verry, J. W. Hornbeck, and C. A. Dolloff (eds.), Riparian Management in Forests of the Continental Eastern United States. Lewis Publishers, Boca Raton, FL.

Radford, A. E., H. E. Ahles, and C. R. Bell. 1968. Manual of the Vascular Flora of the Carolinas. University of North Carolina Press, Chapel Hill, NC. 1183 pp.

Reinert, H. K. 1993. Habitat selection in snakes. Pages 201-240 *in* R. A. Seigel and J.T. Collins (eds.), Snakes: Ecology and Behavior. McGraw Hill, Inc., New York, NY.

31

Ryan, T. J., T. Philippi, Y. A. Leiden, M. E. Dorcas, T. B. Wigley, and J. W. Gibbons. 2002. Monitoring herpetofauna in a managed forest landscape: effects of habitat types and census techniques. Forest Ecology and Management 167:83-90.

Seigel, R. A., and J. W. Gibbons. 1995. Workshop on the ecology, status, and management of the diamondback terrapin (*Malaclemys terrapin*), Savannah River Ecology Laboratory, 2 August 1994: Final results and recommendations. Chelonian Conservation and Biology 1:240-243.

Semlitsch, R. D. 1998. Biological delineation of terrestrial buffer zones for pond-breeding salamanders. Conservation Biology 12:1113-1119.

Semlitsch, R. D. 2003. Conservation of pond-breeding amphibians. Pages. 8-23 *in* R.D. Semlitsch, editor. Amphibian Conservation. Smithsonian Institution Press, Washington, DC.

Semlitsch, R. D., and J. R. Bodie. 1998. Are small, isolated wetlands expendable? Conservation Biology 12:1129-1133.

Semlitsch, R. D., and J. B. Jensen. 2001. Core habitat, not buffer zone. National Wetlands Newsletter 23(4): 5-6, 11.

Tobey, F. J. 1985. Virginia's amphibians and reptiles: A distributional survey. Virginia Herpetological Survey, Virginia Herpetological Society, Purcellville, VA. 114 pp.

Virginia Department of Conservation and Recreation, Division of Natural Heritage. Online database http://www.dcr.virginia.gov/natural_heritage/dbsearchtool.shtml#spp

Whiteman, H. H., T. M. Mills, D. E. Scott, and J. W. Gibbons. 1995. Confirmation of a range extension for the pine woods snake (*Rhadinaea flavilata*). Herpetological Review 26(3):158.

Wright, A. H., and A. A. Wright. 1957. Handbook of Snakes of the United States and Canada. 2 Vols., Cornell University Press, Ithaca, NY. 1105 pp.

Appendix A. Potential checklist of all amphibians and reptiles of George Washington Birthplace National Monument. The checklist is provisional and based on known distributions of amphibians and reptiles in Virginia. It is derived from my master Virginia checklist (unpublished) and from Tobey (1985), Mitchell (1994), and Mitchell and Reay (1999).

Checklist of the Amphibians and Reptiles of George Washington Birthplace National Monument, Virginia

Joseph C. Mitchell

This checklist is based on known distributions of amphibians and reptiles in Maryland.

CLASS AMPHIBIA

Order Anura

Frogs and Toads

Family Bufonidae — Toads

Bufo americanus americanus — Eastern American Toad
Bufo fowleri — Fowler's Toad

Family Microhylidae — Microhylid Frogs

Gastrophryne carolinensis — Eastern Narrow-mouthed Toad

Family Hylidae — Treefrogs

Acris crepitans crepitans — Eastern Cricket Frog
Hyla chrysoscelis — Cope's Gray Treefrog
Hyla cinerea — Green Treefrog
Pseudacris crucifer crucifer — Northern Spring Peeper
Pseudacris feriarum — Upland Chorus Frog

Family Pelobatidae — Spadefoot Toads

Scaphiopus holbrookii — Eastern Spadefoot

Family Ranidae — True Frogs

Rana catesbeiana — American Bullfrog
Rana clamitans melanota — Northern Green Frog
Rana palustris — Pickerel Frog
Rana sphenocephala utricularia — Southern Leopard Frog

Order Caudata

Family Ambystomatidae

    Ambystoma maculatum
    Ambystoma opacum

Family Plethodontidae

    Desmognathus fuscus
    Eurycea cirrigera

    Eurycea guttolineata
    Hemidactylium scutatum
    Plethodon cylindraceus

    Plethodon cinereus
    Pseudotriton montanus montanus
    Pseudotriton ruber ruber

Family Salamandridae

    Notophthalmus viridescens viridescens

Salamanders

Mole Salamanders

Spotted Salamander
Marbled Salamander

Lungless Salamanders

Northern Dusky Salamander
Southern Two-lined Salamander
Three-lined Salamander
Four-toed Salamander
White-spotted Slimy Salamander
Red-backed Salamander
Eastern Mud Salamander
Northern Red Salamander

True Salamanders

Red-spotted Newt

CLASS REPTILIA

Order Testudines

Family Chelydridae

    Chelydra serpentina serpentina

Family Emydidae

    Chrysemys picta picta
    Malaclemys terrapin terrapin

    Pseudemys rubriventris
    Terrapene carolina carolina

Family Kinosternidae

    Kinosternon subrubrum subrubrum
    Sternotherus odoratus

Order Squamata

Turtles

Snapping Turtles

Eastern Snapping Turtle

Pond Turtles

Eastern Painted Turtle
Northern Diamond-backed Terrapin
Northern Red-bellied Cooter
Eastern Box Turtle

Mud and Musk Turtles

Eastern Mud Turtle
Eastern Musk Turtle

Lizards, Snakes and

	Amphisbaenians **Lizards**
Suborder Sauria	
Family Phrynosomatidae	Sceloporine Lizards
Sceloporus undulatus hyacinthinus	Northern Fence Lizard
Family Scincidae	Skinks
Eumeces fasciatus	Five-lined Skink
Eumeces inexpectatus	Southeastern Five-lined Skink
Eumeces laticeps	Broad-headed Skink
Scincella lateralis	Little Brown Skink
Family Teiidae	Tegus and Whiptails
Cnemidophorus sexlineatus sexlineatus	Eastern Six-lined Racerunner
Suborder Serpentes	**Snakes**
Family Colubridae	Colubrids
Carphophis amoenus amoenus	Eastern Wormsnake
Coluber constrictor constrictor	Northern Black Racer
Diadophis punctatus edwardsii	Northern Ring-necked Snake
Elaphe obsoleta obsoleta	Black Ratsnake
Heterodon platirhinos	Eastern Hog-nosed Snake
Lampropeltis calligaster rhombomaculata	Mole Kingsnake
Lampropeltis getula getula	Eastern Kingsnake
Nerodia sipedon sipedon	Northern Watersnake
Opheodrys aestivus	Rough Greensnake
Storeria dekayi dekayi	Northern Brownsnake
Storeria occipitomaculata occipitomaculata	Northern Red-bellied Snake
Thamnophis sauritus sauritus	Eastern Ribbonsnake
Thamnophis sirtalis sirtalis	Eastern Gartersnake
Virginia valeriae valeriae	Eastern Smooth Earthsnake
Family Viperidae	Vipers and Pitvipers
Agkistrodon contortrix mokasen	Northern Copperhead

Appendix B. Amphibian and reptile survey dates and sampling method at George Washington Birthplace National Monument, 2002-2003.

Method	Dates of field trips
VES	**2002**: Mar. 8, 13, 15; Apr. 3, 12, 13, 24; May 23; Jun 3, 18; Jul. 1, 9, 10, 16, 26; Aug. 13, 28; Sep. 5, 11, 30; Oct. 7 -- **2003**: May 1, 21; Jul. 6: Aug. 5
Dipnets	**2002**: Apr. 12; May 23 -- **2003**: May 1; Aug. 5
Minnow traps	**2002**: May 30-31; Jul. 9-10
Turtle traps	**2002**: May 30-31; Jul. 9-10
Road Survey	**2002**: Jul. 26
Audio	**2002**: Mar. 8, 13. 15; Jun. 18 -- 2003: Mar. 22

Appendix C. Diagram of a turtle shell showing the marking scheme for box turtles used on George Washington Birthplace National Monument. The number 159 is indicated by the V-shaped notches filed in the margin of the shell by a triangular file. Combinations of the code numbers yield integers of 1-9. The first four marginals on the anterior left are the digits (1s); the first four on the anterior right are the 10s; the last four marginals on the posterior left are the 100s; and, the last four on the posterior right are the 1000s. Up to 9,999 individuals turtles can be marked using this system.

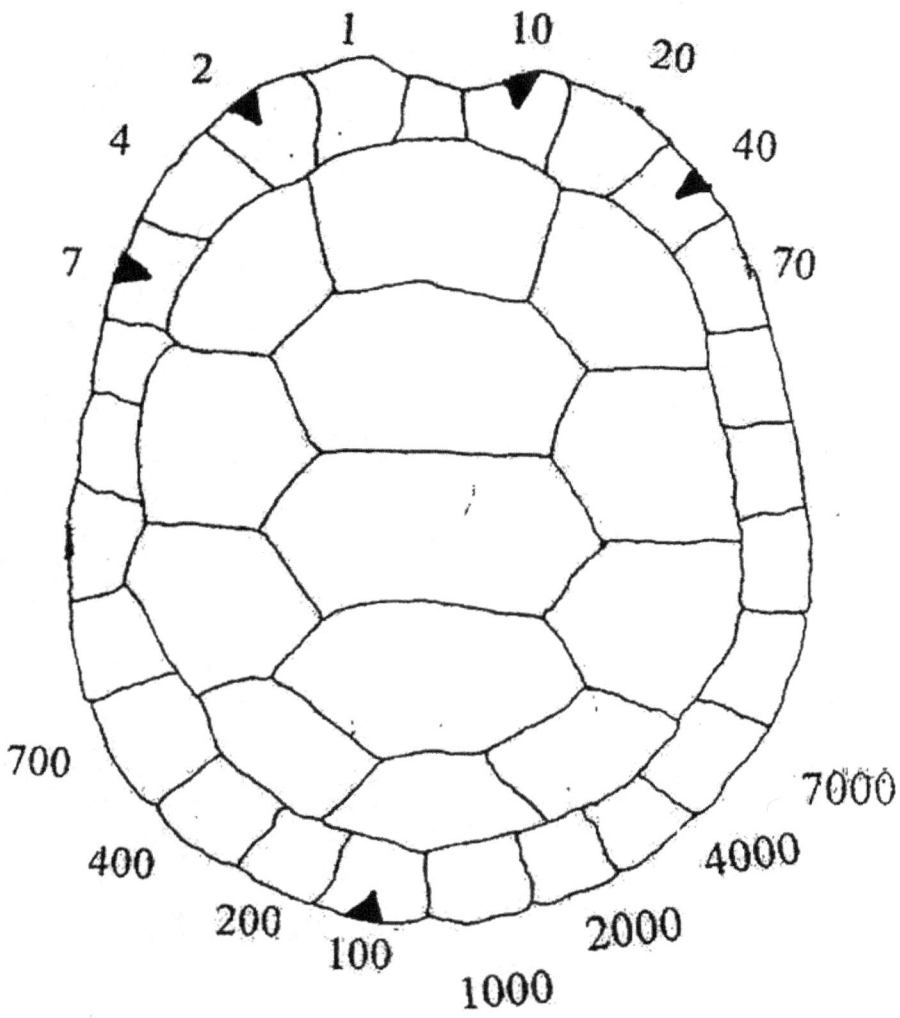

As the nation's primary conservation agency, the Department of the Interior has responsibility for most of our nationally owned public land and natural resources. This includes fostering sound use of our land and water resources; protecting our fish, wildlife, and biological diversity; preserving the environmental and cultural values of our national parks and historical places; and providing for the enjoyment of life through outdoor recreation. The department assesses our energy and mineral resources and works to ensure that their development is in the best interests of all our people by encouraging stewardship and citizen participation in their care. The department also has a major responsibility for American Indian reservation communities and for people who live in island territories under U.S. administration.

NPS D-360 March 2008